# absolutely
# ENTERTAINING!

## ABSOLUTELY ENTERTAINING

ISBN 3-910052-92-4
Library of Congress Catalog Card Number: 96-70275

*First Published in Germany by:*
**Nippan**
**Nippon Shuppan Hanbai**
Deutschland GmbH
Krefelder Str. 85
D-40549 Düsseldorf
Tel   0211/504-8089
Fax   0211/504-9326

*Published by:*
**Supon Design Editions**
1700 K Street, NW, Suite 400
Washington, DC 20006
Tel   202 882 6540
Fax   202 882 6541

Printed in Hong Kong

# absolutely
# ENTERTAINING!

## THE WORLD OF
## ENTERTAINMENT
## GRAPHICS

## SUPON DESIGN GROUP

**Project Director**   Supon Phornirunlit
**Communications Director**   Wayne Kurie
**Publications Director**   Debbi Savitt
**Art Director**   Supon Phornirunlit
**Jacket Designer**   Alexander Chang
**Book Designer**   Alexander Chang
**Editor**   Greg Varner
**Writer**   Linda Klinger
**Agent Representative**   HK Marketing, Los Angeles, CA

*Front Cover Contributors:*
*(Clockwise from top left)*
*Viva Italia!,* Modern Dog, (Page 78)
*Film Collections Logo,* Sabin Design, (Page 31)
*IBM's Olympic Sponsorship Identity,* Supon Design Group, (Page 110)
*"The Four Chinese Beauties" CD Packaging,* Alan Chan Design Company, (Page 46)
*"Working Without Annette" CD Packaging and P.O.P. Display Unit,* Sayles Graphic Design, (Page 60)

*Back Cover Contributors:*
*(Clockwise from top left)*
*"Candles" Video for "Phantom",* Echo Advertising & Marketing Inc., (Page 86)
*Kid's Presentation Brochure,* Laurie Kellihar/World Egg, (Page 13)
*Peacock Music Studio Logo,* DogStar Design, (Page 47)

# table of *CONTENTS*

# intro*DUCTION*

by supon phornirunlit

The willingness, if not eagerness, to be entertained is a universal human trait. One obvious measure of the entertainment industry's importance is its size. Radio and television, movies, music, and theater are bigger today than ever. The last time we checked, Steven Spielberg's movie *Jurassic Park* had grossed over $300 million. Janet Jackson's album *janet* had sold over five million copies. Regional theaters and opera companies were alive and kicking almost everywhere. As you would expect, these separate industries combine to issue a profuse stream of images—images that seep into the most remote corners of the globe. One can find a poster advertising a distant Mozart performance in a tiny European mountain chapel, or an image of singer Michael Jackson painted on the side of a Tanzanian village restaurant. And this mélange of images designed to promote events, concerts, films, and other products requires a high level of both creativity and insight.

"Show business" demands powerful, often emotion-packed graphics to match the flash and intensity of the product. The box office success of many films has been enhanced by posters advertising them in advance. In this merchandising method, posters titillate the audience while withholding the actual product. Film promotions must captivate and even, to a degree, mystify audiences—and also, more and more often, initiate extensive marketing campaigns.

But entertainment graphics are just as often subtle and intensely personal. They can put the intrigue in the first release of an independent film-maker, the emotion in a list of never-before-heard song titles, the electricity in the dark air before the curtain rises on the stage. Design for live theater or book jackets may be classically understated or joltingly experimental.

On T-shirts, posters, playbills, album covers, and elsewhere, graphics propel the excitement of show business. Commercial art can single-handedly draw audiences to an entertainment. Designers in the contemporary music field concur that an awareness of youth interests is critical for attracting audiences to bands targeting younger markets. But an appealing facelift on a classical recording cover can introduce even a baroque piece of music to new, appreciative audiences. As Laurence J. Peter said, "An ounce of image is worth a pound of performance." Design is what can create the image even before the performance is seen.

Just as the annual report and corporate stationery require their own set of approaches, a talk radio program or an avant-garde theater piece uncover their own special challenges. Performing arts, though charged with emotion and personality, can be difficult to define, and even harder to visualize. As Miles Davis once said, "I'll play it first, and tell you what it is later." But when the designer's vision is on-target, few other industries recognize and treasure outstanding graphic design as enthusiastically. The praise for the creative from the creative is a truly worthy compliment.

Designers enjoy working in entertainment for many reasons—most of all, perhaps, the variety of projects that come their way. They can create a realistic stagebill cover for a wrenching drama, and go on to produce impressionistic packaging for a set of commemorative cassettes for an operatic tenor, capturing his character in line and color.

For this book, we've chosen almost 300 of the finest graphics the entertainment industry has offered to date, from a wide variety of projects executed in various styles. They include everything from music store logos to packaging for films on videotape to posters for live theatrical events. We admire these pieces for their insight, originality, depth, and charm.

The entertainment industry gives designers great opportunity for discovering new forms of expression. Whether or not your client list includes well-known names, the pieces featured here will offer you new insights into commercial art. We hope you will be inspired, delighted—and, especially, entertained.

*Supon Phornirunlit is principal of Supon Design Group, where he also serves as creative director. Since founding the studio in 1988, he and his design team have earned more than 600 industry awards, including recognition from every major national design competition. Supon has served on the boards of directors of the Art Director's Club of Metropolitan Washington and the Broadcast Designers' Association, and is a frequent speaker at various industry organizations and universities. The studio's work has been featured in such recognized publications as* Graphis, Communication Arts, Print, Step-by-Step, Studio, *and* How Magazine.

# commen*TARY*

by margo chase / margo chase design

## IT'S A GLAMOUROUS LIFE

Entertainment design seems glamorous. People imagine that you spend your time at catered lunch meetings, gossiping with Madonna. The reality is often far from glamorous.

Music designers are able to do innovative work because the design approval process is limited to one or two people rather than large committees. While some record companies have in-house art departments with many designers and art directors on staff, the musician and one staff designer typically make the design decisions, giving designers room to express the music and themselves. This intimate process can have its drawbacks as well. When the musician is adamant about using some awful painting done by his girlfriend on the cover, there's little a designer can do but groan.

A memorable CD package might inspire a few design junkies to take a risk on something they've never heard, but for the most part, if someone likes the music, they'll buy the CD whether they like the cover or not. This explains why the design budgets for most releases remain small.

Music sales are dependent on radio air play and music videos, so getting the music played on the radio is crucial. This means getting the attention of radio D.J.s and station managers. Because the CD package format is small and all CDs come in the same boring plastic box, it can be difficult to make a particular group stand out. In an attempt to attract attention to new artists or projects, special promotional packaging has evolved. These are elaborately designed, limited edition packages which are sent out to radio station managers and record store buyers. For designers, these projects are a chance to break out of the plastic square and go wild. So much more money and ingenuity goes into the creation of these special packages that the Grammys have had to start a separate category for them.

In the music business, the constant push to stay current can be exhausting, but it also encourages experimentation. Computer graphics technology was quickly embraced by the record business as a way to ease the strain of impossible deadlines and budgets. Programs like Adobe Photoshop have taken costly retouching and image editing out of the lab and into the studio. Layout programs like QuarkXpress have made the process of typesetting and mechanical production seamless. Copy and lyrics from the record company come to the designer on disk. Completed digital mechanicals are sent back to the record company and then go straight to film. While working on a computer has its frustrations, the Macintosh has put more control into the hands of the designer and the results are both weird and wonderful.

Movie campaigns are believed to have a huge impact on the public's perception of a movie and, therefore, on its sales. This brings much more pressure to bear on the designer. For major movies, a studio will typically have several design firms working on the same campaign. The budgets for these presentations are often generous, but the time pressure can be insane. Each firm is expected to present 20 one-sheet ideas in as little as a few days. This gives the designer no time to refine a concept or layout. When you consider that the studio executives who make the design decisions are more concerned with a movie's profitability than the

aesthetics of its campaign, and that an adventurous design is perceived as risky and unsound, you can begin to understand why most movie campaigns look depressingly similar.

To make matters worse, the final approval for any one campaign may rest with committees of businessmen and lawyers who are using the results of market testing, previous movie experience, and the limitations of restrictive contractual agreements to make decisions. Internecine struggles between agents and studio lawyers result in contracts that define design details such as the relative sizes of names in billing blocks or the relationship between the size of art titles and the sizes of various stars' heads. The effect of all of this on the designer is lobotomizing. It's impossible to create a breakthrough poster campaign when one is forced to use five heads of specific sizes on one poster.

To avoid these restrictions, many design firms concentrate their creative energies on the design of teaser posters. These are preliminary posters in a campaign, not limited by the same strict contracts. Movies such as *Batman*

and *Hook* featured teaser posters that were far more compelling than their final one-sheet, because the designers could focus on one iconic image or series of images, rather than being forced to cram everything into a single poster.

While the movie business is a struggle for designers who value self-expression, the process can still be rewarding. Lucrative budgets permit experimentation and the use of technology not available to many. Movie designers were using high-end paint box retouching and image editing long before the Macintosh made computer graphics widely accessible. The budgets and the time pressures also encourage collaboration with other artists, photographers, and designers. Some beautiful work may never see the light of day, but creating it can keep designers going.

Whatever the reality of designing for entertainment, no one has to know you didn't lunch with Madonna.

5

# commen*TARY*

*by robynne raye / modern dog*

### THINGS WE WANTED TO DESIGN AND WHO WE WANTED TO WORK FOR

It was tempting to make up a bunch of high-minded, important-sounding reasons why we went to work in the field of entertainment graphics, but the plain truth is that we just wanted to do posters. As kids, we liked posters and album covers because the artwork on them was cool, and so different from anything else that was presented to us as "art." We all had collections of our favorite pieces and proudly decorated our suburban bedrooms with them. Mike's favorite album cover was Led Zeppelin's *Physical Graffiti*, probably because he's really a Peeping Tom at heart. Later, when we moved to Seattle and started Modern Dog, we were really impressed by all the posters hanging around town—particularly those of Dale Yarger and Art Chantry. Those posters—and the incredible proliferation of them—helped us in our decision to go after theaters as clients. We never thought of ourselves as entering the field of "entertainment graphics," and

we never had a climactic moment pointing us in that direction. Posters seemed like they would be the most fun out of all the kinds of work we felt were accessible to us as a new design firm. We were lucky to secure several theaters as clients right off the bat, and we can truthfully say that theater posters were our bread and butter for many years.

We've probably done more theater posters than any other kind of work, and we've realized a few things that make us like doing them even more. Posters are great because they aren't part of something else. They aren't packaging on top of some product, or a picture introducing a reader to a whole book full of words. Since posters aren't physically connected to what they advertise, they can take on an identity of their own. Precisely because of that, posters are one of the few forms of graphic design that can outlive their original function. In short, we believe that posters document culture. Sounds pretentious, but it's true. The posters that get collected are the ones that represent a certain time or feeling for the person looking at them. And when that happens, posters cross the line from advertising art to a diary of our culture.

But while posters are great, they don't exactly pave the streets with gold. By Modern Dog's second year of business, we had enough theater work to keep us pretty busy, but let's face it, we were starving. We didn't want to do annual reports or corporate brochures, but we sure did want to make rent. So we sat down one afternoon and made lists of what kinds of things we wanted to design and who we wanted to work for. The first list was full of stuff like record covers, candy wrappers, cereal boxes, pinball machines...fun stuff that we'd grown up admiring. The second list—the companies that we wanted to work for—included entertainment conglomerates like MTV, Warner Bros., and Capitol Records, as well as Nike and General Foods. A wide variety of companies selling a wide range of products, but with one thing in common: all of them seemed to have an appreciation for good, fun design (not to mention the budgets to back it up). So we went to work trying to get jobs from those com-

panies. We didn't spend any time developing a marketing plan or figuring out a five-year strategy. We just promoted the hell out of ourselves and stayed in contact with the decision-makers at each company. That's not to say we were irritatingly persistent. We wanted to make our interest and availability known, not bombard anyone with letters or phone calls. But we did send postcards and self-promo goodies, and if we came up with a cool idea for a particular company, we sent it along. After a while, we got to know what people responded to and liked, and they felt comfortable giving us work.

And that brings up the whole subject of self-promotion. Whether the industry targeted is entertainment or manufacturing, self-promotion is about the most important thing a studio can do. We're not talking about a friendly card at Christmas time that says we've donated money to a favorite charity in your name (although that is a very nice thing to do), we're talking about finding the qualities that make us different from any other studio and publicizing them like crazy. We've always felt that our

name and crude (yet friendly) sense of humor were our most unusual attributes, and our self-promotion reflects that. We've come up with some pretty weird pieces, and some people haven't liked them. That's fine with us, because even though someone may not love our fur box, it certainly stands out. The pieces that are borderline obnoxious are the ones that are remembered most. And if it gets us a job we want or makes someone laugh, it's worth the risk. We see too many pieces of self-promotion that are about as risky as a pancake. I mean really, who's going to hire you if your stuff looks like everyone else's, and you didn't even include candy?

# air*WAVES*

## absolutely

**R**adio and television have the ability to focus tightly on world events and on your five-square-mile township. With the advent of cable, generations are growing up with a buffet selection of entertainment, from situation comedies to operettas, and with instant infomation. Telephones make many programs interactive. Some of the most interesting designs relating to these media are included here, from annual reports for networks to promotional pieces for programs to videos.

**Title**  ESPN Video Promos
**Design Firm**  Kampah Visions
**Art Directors**  Flavio Kampah,
 Phil Delbourgo
**Designer**  Flavio Kampah
**Client**  Big Fat TV

10

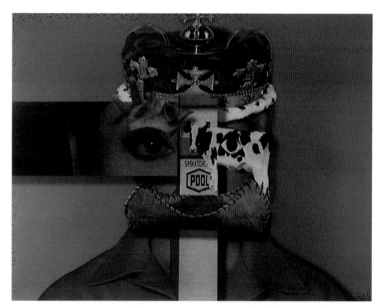
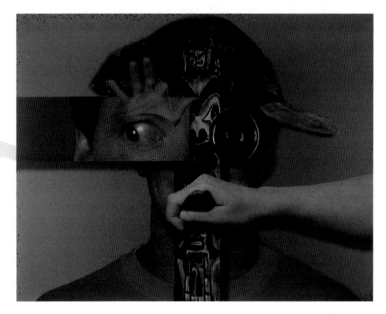
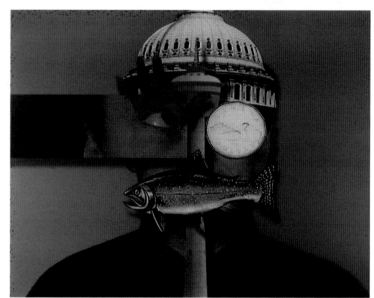

**Title** "Royal Canadian Air Farce" Video
**Design Firm** Canadian Broadcasting
     Corporation
**Art Director** Tony Cleave
**Designer** Tony Cleave
**Client** Royal Canadian Air Farce

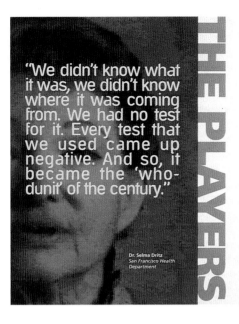

## THE PLAYERS

"We didn't know what it was, we didn't know where it was coming from. We had no test for it. Every test that we used came up negative. And so, it became the 'who-dunit' of the century."

**Dr. Selma Dritz**
*San Francisco Health Department*

Y

*A Time of AIDS* features interviews with a wide range of key people who have been on the front lines fighting the epidemic, including:

**Dr. Robert Gallo,** the former head of AIDS research at the National Institutes of Health who became involved in a highly controversial race with the French to identify the AIDS virus;

**Dr. Luc Montagnier,** head of the Pasteur Institute's AIDS research team, who pioneered the French effort to find the AIDS virus;

**Dr. Don Francis,** the government scientist with the Centers for Disease Control whose job it was to work out how to control the spread of AIDS, and **Dr. James Curran,** former director of AIDS research at the CDC;

**Roger McFarlane** and **Larry Kramer,** founders of the Gay Men's Health Crisis and two of the first gay activists to mobilize the gay community against AIDS;

**Dr. Selma Dritz** of the San Francisco Health Department, one of the first people to recognize the onslaught of what would become known as AIDS;

**Surgeon General C. Everett Koop,** the top health official in the Reagan Administration;

**Dr. Anthony Fauci,** who oversaw the government's testing of experimental AIDS drugs.

The series also interviews the people most directly affected – AIDS victims, their families and loved ones – to provide a very personal view of the emotional effects of the disease.

[ The highly-charged real-life drama behind the AIDS epidemic is revealed as never before. The tragic stories behind the headlines come to life, including the hunt for the AIDS virus that turned prominent American and French researchers into intense and controversial rivals; the fatal decision by blood banks not to screen donors for infected blood until months after a test became available; the beginnings of the gay activist movement as a reaction to government inertia and cultural stereotyping; the black-market use of experimental AIDS drugs and the dispute surrounding the marketing of the ultimately unsuccessful "wonder drug" AZT.

"As early as October of 1984, the blood bankers knew... that there were infected people walking in the door... no did not change what they were doing until the ... licensed on March ...

**Dr. Marcus Conant**
*Former Director of The AIDS Clinical Research Center, University of California, San Francisco.*

## THE CONTROVERSIES

... arly seen as a gay disease, as self-... d there were tremendous problems ... ople to accept that these people ... treated like any other patients... ... medicine maybe 600 years ago.

**Dr. Michael Adler**
*Head of Venereal Disease Section Middlesex Hospital, Great Britain*

## A TIME OF AIDS

DISCOVERY JOURNAL FOUR-PART MINI-SERIES,

TELLS THE REAL STORY BEHIND THE

EPIDEMIC THAT CHANGED THE WORLD.

**JOURNAL** Discovery

**Title**  "A Time of AIDS" Press Kit

**Design Firm**  Discovery Design Group, Discovery Communications, Inc.

**Art Director**  Larnie Higgins

**Designer**  Larnie Higgins, Richard Lee Heffner

**Client**  The Discovery Design Channel, Discovery Communications, Inc.

11

12

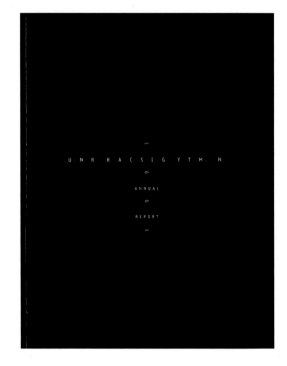

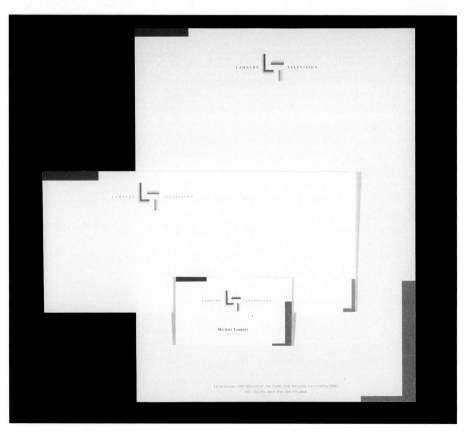

*Top*

**Title**   1993 Turner Broadcast System, Inc.
             Report
**Design Firm**   Corporate Reports
**Art Director**   Brant Day
**Designer**   Kitsie Riggall
**Client**   Turner Broadcasting

*Bottom*

**Title**   Lambert Television Logo and
             Stationery
**Design Firm**   White & Associates
**Art Director**   Trina Nuovo
**Designer**   Byron Lee
**Client**   Lambert Television

*absolutely*

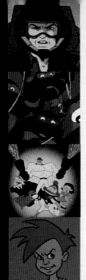

## USA CARTOON EXPRESS

On weekday and Sunday mornings, and early fringe, you'll find kids across the nation catching the USA Cartoon Express, their TV ticket to today's animated favorites. From GI Joe to Teenage Mutant Ninja Turtles, USA's got the classic characters and contemporary cartoons that young people want most. For 28 1/2 hours each week, cartoon blocks on USA feature hot titles like Scooby Doo, Terrytoons, Chipmunks Go to the Movies, Ghostbusters, and Super Mario Bros. 3. They all add up to the most-watched daily cartoon block on cable!

## ORIGINAL PROGRAMMING

USA Cartoon Express is speeding into the future with investment in new original kids' programming:

ITSY BITSY SPIDER

A tiny four-eyed, six-legged spider who avenges insect injustice, Itsy overcomes odds to save the day — whether he's liberating kids from a maniacal karate instructor or wreaking havoc on a TV cooking show! Itsy Bitsy Spider features the voices of The Facts of Life's Charlotte Rae and Max Headroom's Matt Frewer. It's a USA exclusive!

PROBLEM CHILD

In a world full of grown-ups, mind-boggling mischief rules, as Junior torments the neighborhood doctor's office, locks himself in the bathroom and gets a Presidential appointment! Seen exclusively on USA, Problem Child is based on the hit Hollywood comedy film of the same name.

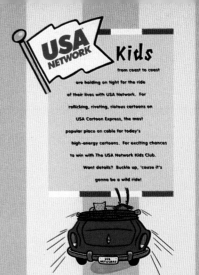

## USA NETWORK Kids

from coast to coast are holding on tight for the ride of their lives with USA Network. For rollicking, riveting, riotous cartoons on USA Cartoon Express, the most popular place on cable for today's high-energy cartoons. For exciting chances to win with The USA Network Kids Club. Want details? Buckle up, 'cause it's gonna be a wild ride!

---

# IT'S A WILD RIDE...

## KID-TESTED TV FAVORITES: DRIVING THE SUCCESS OF CHILDREN'S PROGRAMMING

---

## SCI-FI CARTOON QUEST

On weekday and Saturday mornings, kids beam up Sci-Fi Cartoon Quest, the only block on cable devoted to science fiction animation. Kids leap into the future with a brave new world of sci-fi cartoons like Terrahawks, Star Wars Droids: The Adventures of R2-D2 and C-3PO, Ewoks, Transformers, The New Adventures of Gigantor, Land of the Lost, Little Shop, Laser Patrol, Galaxy High School, Fantastic Voyage, and the animated version of Star Trek (featuring the voices of the original series cast). It's six days a week of far-out fun!

## COSMIC CREW

Here's an added value opportunity for the next millennium: Cosmic Crew, a promotional tool with astronomical potential! Like USA Network's highly successful Kids Club, the Sci-Fi Channel's interactive Cosmic Crew vignettes give kids fun chances to play for prizes. Each Cosmic Crew vignette is specifically customized and exclusively produced to fit advertisers' special needs. Lift off with Cosmic Crew to reach today's young sci-fi fans; it's a unique new vehicle to showcase products!

### SCI-FI CHANNEL KIDS PROGRAMMING SCHEDULE

| Monday - Friday | |
|---|---|
| 6AM-9AM ET* | SCI-FI CARTOON QUEST |
| Saturday | |
| 7AM-11AM ET* | SCI-FI CARTOON QUEST |

**Title**   Kid's Presentation Brochure
**Design Firm**   Laurie Kellihar/World Egg
**Art Director**   Elisa Feinman
**Designer**   Laurie Kellihar
**Client**   USA Networks

14

**Title**   "Duckman Mailer" Promotion
**Design Firm**   Diagraphics
**Art Director**   Elisa Feinman
**Designer**   Diagraphics
**Client**   USA Networks

*Top*

**Title**   PBS Radio – FM Promotion
**Design Firm**   Value Added Design Pty
**Art Director**   Heather Towns
**Designer**   Heather Towns
**Client**   PBS Radio – FM

*Bottom*

**Title**   FOX Broadcasting '93-'94
　　　　　New Season Brochure
**Design Firm**   CBO
**Art Director**   John O'Brien
**Designer**   John O'Brien
**Client**   FOX Broadcasting

15

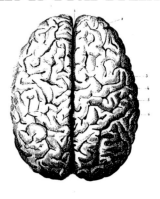

# This Is Your Brain.

# This Is Your Brain On BEAKMAN.

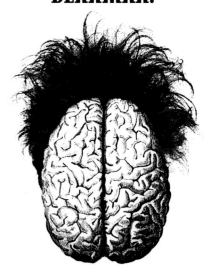

## BEAKMAN'S WORLD

Everything you ever
wanted to know but didn't
know whom to ask.

*Left*

**Title**   Sci-Fi Satellite Gear Promotion
**Design Firm**   Peter Millen Design
**Art Director**   Elisa Feinman
**Designer**   Peter Millen
**Client**   USA Networks

*Right*

**Title**   "Beakman's World" –
            Brain on Beakman Ad
**Design Firm**   Columbia Pictures
            Television Distribution
**Art Director**   Ellen Stefani
**Designer**   Ron Taft
**Client**   Beakman's World

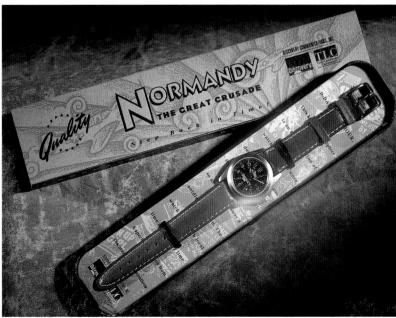

**Title** "Normandy: The Great Crusade" Premiums

**Design Firm** Discovery Design Group, Discovery Communications, Inc.

**Art Director** Richard Lee Heffner

**Designer** Richard Lee Heffner

**Client** The Discovery Channel, Discovery Communications, Inc.

17

ART LIBRARY

*absolutely*

*Top*

**Title**   Upfront Ad Sales Materials

**Design Firm**   Discovery Design Group
Discovery Communications, Inc.

**Art Director**   Larnie Higgins

**Designers**   Richard Lee Heffner,
Mark Scheider

**Client**   Discovery Communications, Inc.

*Bottom*

**Title**   Media Kit for Entertainment Weekly

**Design Firm**   Platinum Design, Inc.

**Art Director**   S. Quinn

**Designer**   S. Quinn

**Client**   Entertainment Weekly

**Title**  "30 Fragments 60 Fields" Promotion
**Design Firm**  Kampah Visions
**Art Director**  Flavio Kampah
**Designer**  Flavio Kampah
**Client**  Radius

20

**Title**   BET Affiliate Sales Promotion
**Design Firm**   Supon Design Group, Inc.
**Creative Director**   Scott Perkins
**Art Directors**   Supon Phornirunlit,
        Andrew Dolan
**Designer**   Andrew Berman
**Project Directors**   LaTanya Butler,
        Angela Scott, Matilda Ivey
**Client**   Black Entertainment Television

**Title**  Western Channel Promotion
**Design Firm**  Colorado Production Group
**Art Director**  Jeanne Kopeck
**Designer**  Jeanne Kopeck
**Editor**  Colin Spencer
**Music**  Daniel Clason
**Client**  Encore

22

**Title** "Inside Washington" Program Open

**Design Firm** W*USA-TV Design
Department

**Art Director** Mary Ruesen Strauss

**Designers** Mary Ruesen Strauss,
Donna Beard

**Animators** Donna Beard, Scott Suess

**Client** W*USA-TV

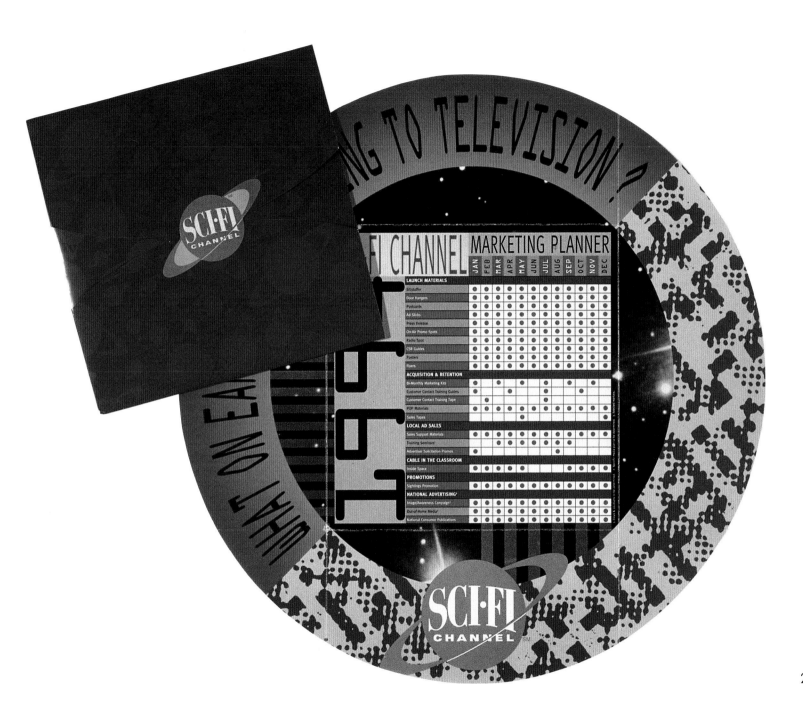

23

**Title**  Sci-Fi Western Show Brochure
**Design Firm**  Peter Millen Design
**Art Director**  Elisa Feinman
**Designer**  Peter Millen
**Client**  USA Networks

24

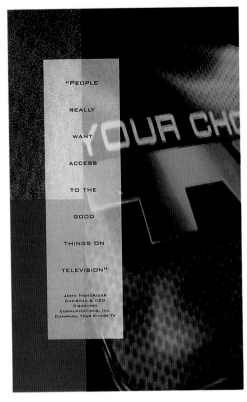

*absolutely*

**Title**  Your Choice TV Letterhead and Brochure
**Design Firm**  Supon Design Group, Inc.
**Creative Director**  Gil Cowley
**Art Directors**  Supon Phornirunlit,
 Andrew Dolan
**Designers**  Apisak Saibua, Richard Boynton
**Project Director**  Kathleen Hayes
**Client**  Your Choice TV

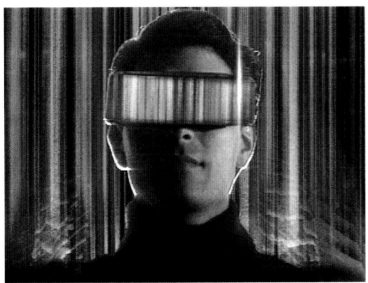

**Title**  "Virtual Reality" TV News Promotion
**Design Firm**  W*USA-TV Design Department
**Art Director**  Mary Ruesen Strauss
**Designer**  Mary Ruesen Strauss
**Animator**  Karen Swenholt
**Producer**  Mag Cumbow
**Client**  W*USA-TV

*absolutely*

**Title**   "La Presse Sort II" Commercial Video
**Design Firm**   Big Bang Technologies, Inc.
**Art Directors**   Pierre Drovin,
        BCP Agency
**Producer**   Danny Bergeron
**Director**   Danny Bergeron
**Production**   Big Bang Technologies
**Client**   BCP Montreal

BET On Jazz: The Cable Jazz Channel™ is a new 24-hour, advertiser-supported, basic cable network. The channel will present jazz and its many dynamic styles in an effort to capture the interest of a loyal audience and create enthusiasm for televised jazz entertainment.

...BET On Jazz: The Cable ...tive and creatively exciting ... hours daily, we hope to ... and enjoyment to the ... birth to an outlet that will ... most highly regarded and ... in the world.

...Jazz Channel, we will bring ...s: exciting newcomers, ... more. We look forward to ...relationships with the cable ...BET On Jazz: The Cable Jazz Channel

**Title** BET on Jazz Brochure
**Design Firm** Supon Design Group, Inc.
**Creative Director** Scott Perkins
**Art Directors** Supon Phornirunlit, Andrew Dolan
**Designer** Anthony Fletcher
**Photo Research** PhotoAssist, Inc.
**Project Directors** LaTanya Butler,
**Client** Black Entertainment Television

27

# cine*MATIC*

*absolutely*

**G**ather a crowd, turn out the lights, and project moving images on the wall—presto! Everyone dreams the same dream. While the magic of cinema is undeniable, it's a real challenge to capture this hocus-pocus graphically. Here are some of the most successful attempts we've discovered, from personal logos to studio promotions to covers for books about the industry to the beloved film poster. Presto! We're pleased to show you the magic of good film-related design.

**Title**  The Rainy States Film Festival Poster
**Design Firm**  Modern Dog
**Art Director**  George Estrada
**Designer**  George Estrada
**Illustrator**  George Estrada
**Client**  The Rainy States Film Festival

30

absolutely

**Title** Once Upon a Time in China II
Poster
**Design Firm** Alan Chan Design
Company
**Art Director** Alan Chan
**Designers** Alan Chan, Peter Lo
**Client** Film Workshop, Ltd.

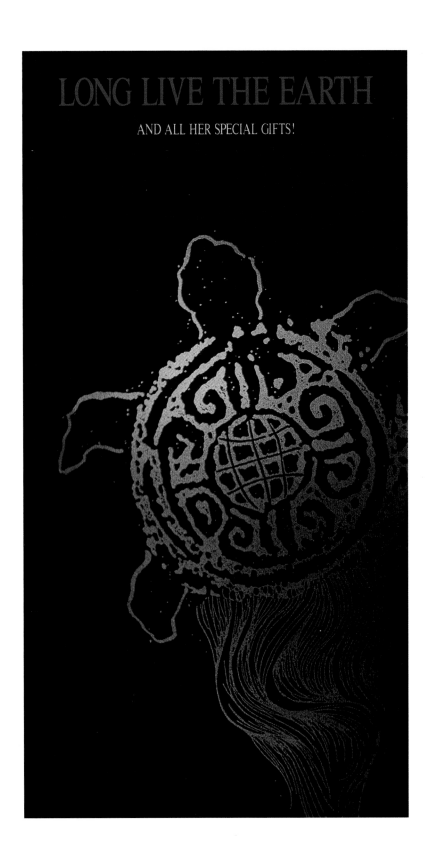

**LONG LIVE THE EARTH**

AND ALL HER SPECIAL GIFTS!

*Left*
**Title**   Earth Vision Film Festival
           Promotion
**Design Firm**   Douglas Design
**Art Director**   Douglas Doolittle
**Designer**   Douglas Doolittle
**Client**   Urban Communications

*Right*
**Title**   Film Collections Logo
**Design Firm**   Sabin Design
**Art Director**   Alison Hill
**Designer**   Tracy Sabin
**Client**   Turner Entertainment Co.

31

32  **Title**  "Heaven and Earth" Promotional Film Identity
**Design Firm**  Tim Girvin Design, Inc.
**Art Director**  Tim Girvin
**Designer**  Tim Girvin
**Client**  Seiniger Advertising

**Title**  Rim Films Logo
**Design Firm**  PPA Design Limited
**Art Director**  Byron Jacobs
**Designer**  Byron Jacobs
**Photographer**  Ted Chin
**Client**  Golden Harvest

**Title**  Jeanne Evans/Actress Logo
**Design Firm**  John Evans Design
**Art Director**  John Evans
**Designer**  John Evans
**Client**  Jeanne Evans

*Left*

**Title**   "Boat People" Film Poster

**Design Firm**   PPA Design Limited

**Art Director**   Byron Jacobs

**Designers**   Byron Jacobs, Michelle Shek

**Client**   Golden Harvest

*Right*

**Title**   "Top Squad" Film Poster

**Design Firm**   PPA Design Limited

**Art Director**   Byron Jacobs

**Designers**   Byron Jacobs, Michelle Shek

**Client**   Golden Harvest

34

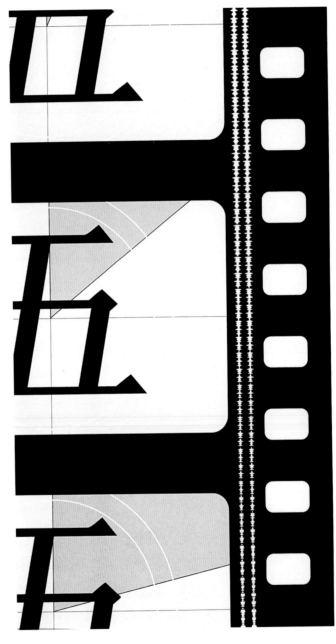

Golden Harvest
congratulates
The Fifth
Tokyo International
Film Festival

Golden Harvest

*Left*

**Title** "King of Chess" Promotion

**Design Firm** Alan Chan Design Company

**Art Director** Alan Chan

**Designers** Alan Chan, Alvin Chan, Chen Shun Tsoi

**Client** Film Workshop Co., Ltd.

*Right*

**Title** Fifth Tokyo International Film Festival Advertisement

**Design Firm** PPA Design Limited

**Art Director** Byron Jacobs

**Designer** Michelle Shek

**Client** Golden Harvest

*absolutely*

*Top*

**Title**   "Hello, I Must Be Going" Book
**Design Firm**   Carol Publishing Group
**Art Director**   Steven Brower
**Designer**   Steven Brower
**Client**   Carol Publishing Group

*Bottom*

**Title**   "The Three Stooges Scrapbook"
**Design Firm**   Carol Publishing Group
**Art Director**   Steven Brower
**Designer**   Steven Brower
**Client**   Carol Publishing Group

35

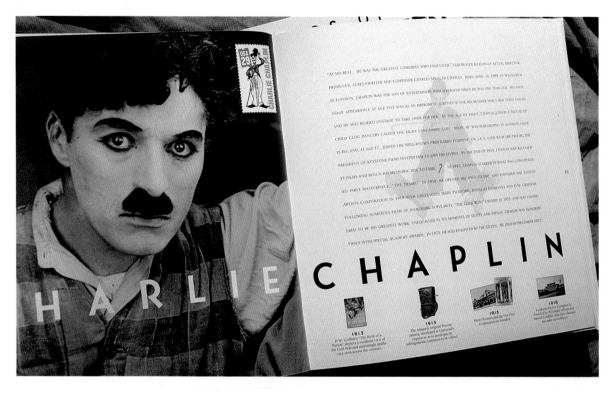

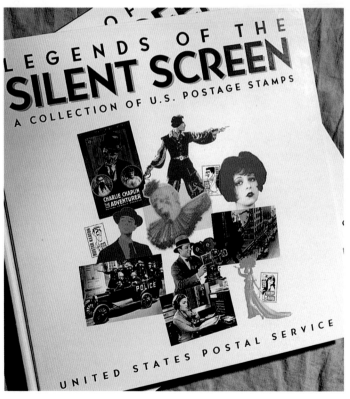

absolutely

**Title**   "Legends of the Silent Screen" Book
**Design Firm**   Supon Design Group, Inc.
**Creative Director**   Terry McCaffrey
**Art Directors**   Supon Phornirunlit, Andrew Dolan
**Designers**   Apisak Saibua, Andrew Berman,
            Dianne Cook, Richard Boynton
**Editor**   Linda Klinger
**Photo Research**   PhotoAssist, Inc.
**Client**   U. S. Postal Service

**Title**  Films from the Fringe Poster
**Design Firm**  Supon Design Group, Inc.
**Art Directors**  Supon Phornirunlit, Andrew Dolan
**Designer**  Andrew Dolan
**Project Director**  Terry McCaffrey
**Client**  American Institute of Graphic Arts

*Left*

**Title**  "Sex and Zen" Film Poster
**Design Firm**  PPA Design Limited
**Art Director**  Byron Jacobs
**Designer**  Byron Jacobs
**Client**  Golden Harvest

*Right*

**Title**  "Actress" Poster
**Design Firm**  PPA Design Limited
**Art Director**  Byron Jacobs
**Designers**  Byron Jacobs, Tracy Hoi
**Client**  Golden Harvest

39

Title   Golden Harvest 1992 New Year's Card
Design Firm   PPA Design Limited
Art Director   Byron Jacobs
Designers   Byron Jacobs, Tracy Hoi
Client   Golden Harvest

*absolutely*

*Top*
**Title** "Blown Away" Book
**Design Firm** Mike Salisbury
Communications
**Art Director** Mike Salisbury
**Designers** Mike Salisbury, Patrick O'Neal
**Client** MGM

*Bottom*
**Title** "The Fly" Logo
**Design Firm** Mike Salisbury
Communications, Inc.
**Art Director** Mike Salisbury
**Designer** Mike Salisbury
**Client** 20th Century Fox

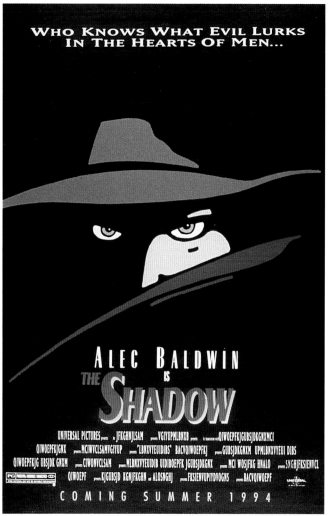

Left
**Title** "Younger & Younger" Poster
**Design Firm** Wueschner, Rohwer
**Art Director** Petra Barchfeld
**Designer** Andreas Rintzner
**Client** Jugendfilm/Berlin

41

Right
**Title** "The Shadow" Poster
**Design Firm** Mike Salisbury Communications
**Art Director** Mike Salisbury
**Designer** Mike Salisbury
**Client** Universal

*Top*

**Title**  Illinois Film Office Location Guide
**Design Firm**  Kym Abrams Design, Inc.
**Design Firm for Film Logo**  Zechman Associates
**Art Director**  Kym Abrams
**Designer**  Mike Stees
**Designer for Film Logo**  Dick Lemon
**Client**  Illinois Film Office

*Bottom*

**Title**  "Meteor Man" Logo
**Design Firm**  Mike Salisbury Communications
**Art Director**  Mike Salisbury
**Designer**  Mike Salisbury
**Client**  MGM

**Title** "To Live and Die in L.A." Poster
**Design Firm** Mike Salisbury Communications
**Art Director** Mike Salisbury
**Designer** Mike Salisbury
**Client** MGM

# tune*FUL*

## *absolutely*

**M**usic's roots reach back to the first human beings beating rhythms on a hollowed-out tree. Like the Olympic Games or a kiss, it does not need translation to be enjoyed. Various ways have been discovered to combine sounds, notes and tones into something lyrical, stimulating, haunting, and powerful. Music has incorporated words, bells, whistles, cannons, and computers. Here, we bring you some of the most successful designs influenced by this experimentation with sound.

45

**Title**  Jazz Festival Willisau '93 Poster
**Design Firm**  Niklaus Troxler
**Art Director and Designer**
    Niklaus Troxler
**Client**  Jazz in Willisau

*absolutely*

46

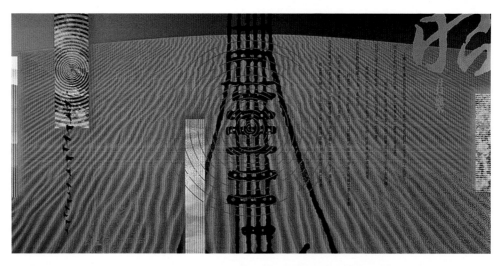

**Title** "The Four Chinese Beauties"
CD Packaging
**Design Firm** Alan Chan Design
Company
**Art Director** Alan Chan
**Designers** Alan Chan, Alvin Chan,
Cetric Leung
**Client** James Wong Productions Ltd.

**POLYDOR**

**Title** Polydor Logo
**Design Firm** Jay Vigon Studio
**Art Director** Jay Vigon
**Designer** Jay Vigon
**Client** Polydor

**Title** Peacock Music Studio Logo
**Design Firm** DogStar Design
**Art Director** Rodney Davidson
**Designer** Rodney Davidson
**Illustrator** Rodney Davidson
**Client** Peacock Music Studio

**Title** Gregory Freeze, Singer/Pianist Logo
**Design Firm** DogStar Design
**Art Director** Rodney Davidson
**Designer** Rodney Davidson
**Illustrator** Rodney Davidson
**Client** Gregory Freeze

48

*absolutely*

*Top*

**Title**   Urbanized/Helpless CD Packaging

**Design Firm**   PolyGram Records

**Art Director**   Michael A. Klotz

**Designer**   Michael A. Klotz

**Client**   Mercury

*Bottom*

**Title**   Ethyl Meatplow/"Happy Days,
            Sweetheart" CD Packaging

**Design Firm**   Derailed Design Group

**Art Director**   Skiles

**Designer**   Skiles

**Photographer**   Exum

**Calligrapher**   Nancy Ogami

**Client**   Dali Records

*Top*

**Title**  Lou Reed/"Magic and Loss"—Metal
Memorial Edition CD Packaging
**Design Firm**  Just Design
**Art Directors**  Sylvia Reed, Spencer Drate
**Designers**  Sylvia Reed, Spencer Drate,
Jütka Salavetz, Dennis Ascienzo
**Photographer**  Louis James
**Client**  Sire/Warner Bros.

*Bottom*

**Title**  Berserk CD Packaging
**Design Firm**  Supon Design Group, Inc.
**Art Director**  Andrew Dolan
**Designer**  Andrew Dolan
**Client**  Go-Kart Records

49

*absolutely*

*Top*
**Title**  Joice Walton CD Packaging
**Design Firm**  Tollner Design Group
**Art Director**  Jeff Dentino
**Designer**  Christopher Canote
**Printer**  A's Printing
**Client**  Pinnacle Records

*Bottom*
**Title**  South by Southwest Music Convention Ad
**Design Firm**  Modern Dog
**Art Director**  Laurie Burke
**Designer**  Michael Strassburger
**Copywriter**  Michael Strassburger
**Client**  Warner Bros. Records

**Title** The Indians/Indianism CD Packaging
**Design Firm** PolyGram Records
**Art Director** Sheryl Lutz-Brown
**Designer** Sheryl Lutz-Brown
**Client** PolyGram Records

52

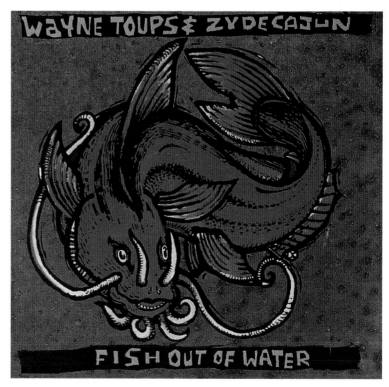

*absolutely*

*Top*

**Title**   Wayne Toups & Zydecajun/Fish Out of
              Water CD Packaging

**Design Firm**   PolyGram Records

**Art Director**   Michael Bays

**Designer**   Michael A. Klotz

**Illustrator**   Donald Klotz, Jr.

**Client**   Wayne Toups

*Bottom*

**Title**   Yoko Owada "Evening of Mozart" Poster

**Design Firm**   Hiromura Design Office

**Art Director**   Massaki Hiromura

**Designers**   Massaki Hiromura,
                 Takafumi Kusagaya

**Client**   Million Concert Company, Ltd.

*Top*
**Title** Shou Dú CD Packaging
**Design Firm** Alan Chan Design Company
**Art Director** Alan Chan
**Designers** Alan Chan, Peter Lo
**Client** Music Factory

*Bottom*
**Title** Shou Dú Poster
**Design Firm** Alan Chan Design Company
**Art Director** Alan Chan
**Designers** Alan Chan, Peter Lo
**Client** Music Factory

53

54

*absolutely*

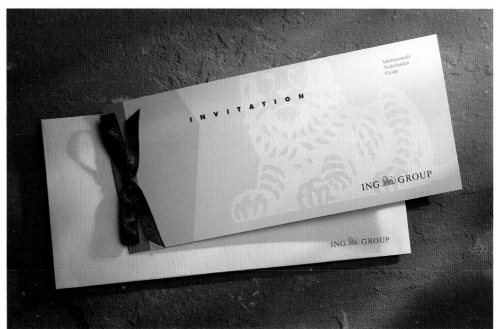

**Title**  Royal Concertgebouw Orchestra Invitation
and Program
**Design Firm**  Leslie Chan Design Co. Ltd.
**Art Director**  Chan Wing Kei.Leslie
**Designers**  Chan Wing Kei.Leslie,
Tong Song Wei
**Client**  Ing Bank

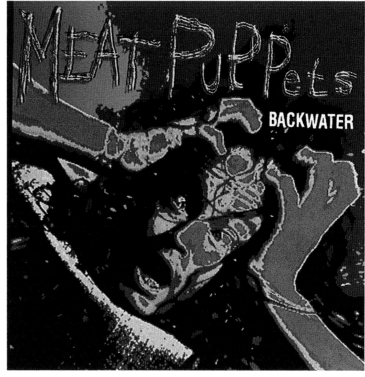

*Top*

**Title**   Meat Puppets/Backwater CD Packaging
**Design Firm**   PolyGram Records
**Art Director**   Michael A. Klotz
**Designer**   Michael A. Klotz
**Client**   Meat Puppets

*Bottom*

**Title**   Natraj/"Meet Me Anywhere" CD Cover
**Design Firm**   design M design W
**Art Directors**   James Westhall,
  Maureen Maloney
**Designers**   James Westhall, Maureen Maloney
**Digital Imaging**   Paul Roseneck
**Calligrapher**   Maureen Maloney
**Client**   Dorian Group, Ltd.

55

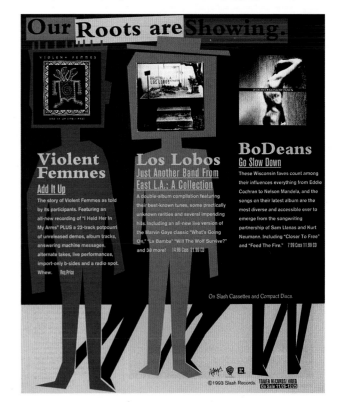

*absolutely*

*Top*

**Title**   Utah Symphony 50th Anniversary Program
**Design Firm**   Richards & Swensen, Inc.
**Art Director**   William Swensen
**Designers**   William Swensen, Michael Richards
**Photographer**   Dirk Douglass
**Client**   Utah Symphony

*Bottom*

**Title**   Our Roots Are Showing Billboard Ad
**Design Firm**   Modern Dog
**Art Director**   Kim Champagne
**Designer**   Vittorio Costarella
**Illustrator**   Vittorio Costarella
**Client**   Warner Bros. Records

57

ART LIBRARY

58

1. Buju Banton/"*Red Rose*" . . . . . . . . . from the LP, CT & CD - Voice Of Jamaica, 314 518 013-1/4/2, in-store 8/3/93.

2. Buju Banton/"*Deportees (Things Change)*" . . . . . . from the LP, CT & CD - Voice Of Jamaica, 314 518 013-1/4/2

3. Third World/"*Mi Legal (Massive Lady Venus Mix)*" original version on the CT & CD - Committed, 314 510 279-4/2

4. David Morales & The Bad Yard Club/"*Gimme Luv (Eenie Meenie Miny Mo)(Dancehall Edit)*" . . . . . . . . . . . . . . . . . . . . . . . . . . . . . . . original version found on the LP, CT & CD - The Program, 314 518 015-1/4/2, in-store 7/20/93.

5. Tony Toni Toné/"*Dancehall*" . . . . . . . . . . . . . from the CT, CD & DCC - Sons Of Soul, 314 514 933-4/2/5

6. Joe/"*I'm In Luv (E-Smoove Raw Edit)*" . . . . . . from the CT & CD - Everything, 314 518 016-4/2, in-store 8/3/93

7. David Morales & The Bad Yard Club/"*In De Ghetto*" . . . . . . . . . . . . . . . . . . . . . . . . . . . . . . . . . . from the LP, CT & CD - The Program, 314 518 015-1/4/2, in-store 7/20/93.

8. Buju Banton/"*Operation Ardent*" . . . . . from the LP, CT & CD - Voice Of Jamaica, 314 518 013-1/4/2, in-store 8/3/93.

9. Third World/"*Reggae Ambassadors*" . . . . . . . . . . . . . . . . from the forthcoming Chronicles Deluxe Anthology.

**Title**   150 Proof Riddims CD Packaging
**Design Firm**   PolyGram Records
**Art Director**   Michael A. Klotz
**Designer**   Michael A. Klotz
**Client**   Mercury

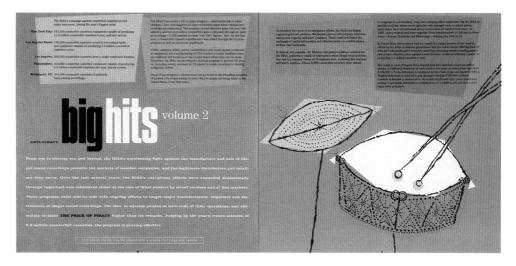

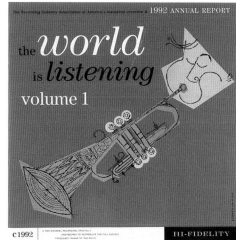

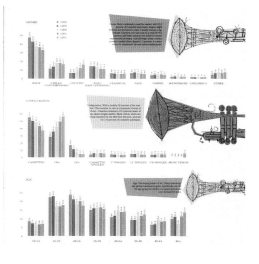

**Title** "The World is Listening" Annual Report

**Design Firm** Recording Industry Association of America

59

**Art Director** Neil Ashby

**Designer** Neil Ashby

**Illustrator** Dave Plunkert

**Photographer** Barb Kinney

**Client** Recording Industry Association of America

*Left*

**Title**  Together For the Cure Invitation
**Design Firm**  Platinum Design, Inc.
**Art Directors**  Sandra Quinn, Vickie Peslack
**Designer**  Sandra Quinn
**Client**  AMFAR Foundation

*Right*

**Title**  "Working Without Annette" CD Packaging
and P.O.P. Display Unit
**Design Firm**  Sayles Graphic Design
**Art Director**  John Sayles
**Designer**  John Sayles
**Client**  The Flying Marsupials

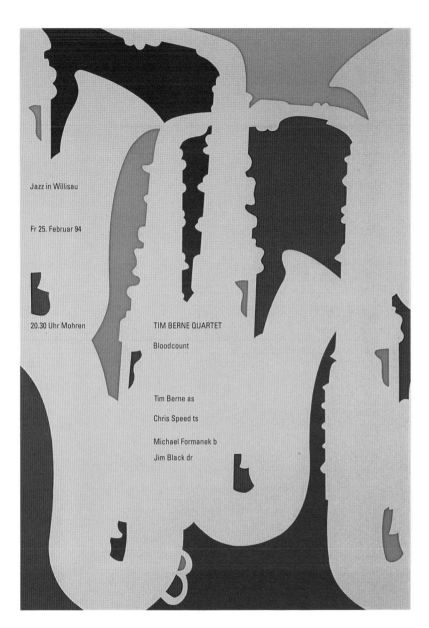

Jazz in Willisau

Fr 25. Februar 94

20.30 Uhr Mohren

TIM BERNE QUARTET

Bloodcount

Tim Berne as

Chris Speed ts

Michael Formanek b

Jim Black dr

*Left*

**Title**  Jazz Festival Willisau '93 Poster
**Design Firm**  Niklaus Troxler
**Art Director**  Niklaus Troxler
**Designer**  Niklaus Troxler
**Client**  Jazz in Willisau

*Right*

**Title**  Love + Rockets
**Design Firm**  Modern Dog
**Art Director**  Vittorio Castarella
**Designer**  Vittorio Castarella
**Illustrator**  Vittorio Castarella
**Client**  Tasty Shows

*absolutely*

**Title** "Even Better Than The Real Thing"
Music Video
**Design Firm** Kampah Visions
**Art Director** Flavio Kampah
**Designer** Flavio Kampah
**Client** U2

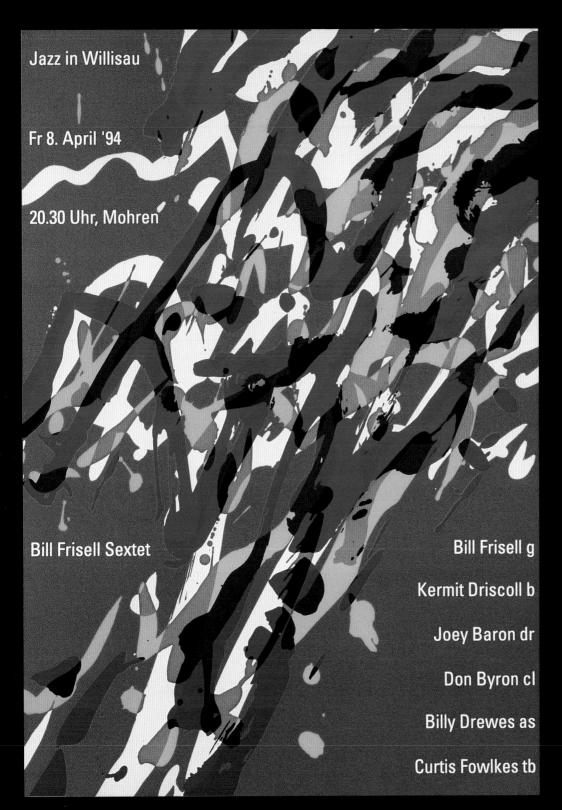

Jazz in Willisau

Fr 8. April '94

20.30 Uhr, Mohren

Bill Frisell Sextet

Bill Frisell g

Kermit Driscoll b

Joey Baron dr

Don Byron cl

Billy Drewes as

Curtis Fowlkes tb

63

**Title**  Bill Frisell Sextet Ehrilich Quartet Poster
**Design Firm**  Niklaus Troxler
**Art Director**  Niklaus Troxler
**Designer**  Niklaus Troxler
**Client**  Jazz in Willisau

64

_absolutely_

**Title** Marty Ehrlich Quartet Poster
**Design Firm** Niklaus Troxler
**Art Director** Niklaus Troxler
**Designer** Niklaus Troxler
**Client** Jazz in Willisau

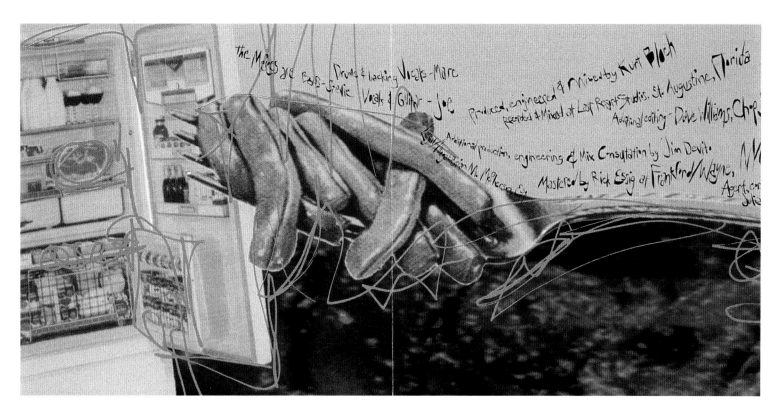

**Title** Meices/Tastes Like Chicken
CD Packaging
**Design Firm** PolyGram Records
**Designer** Patricia Lie
**Illustrator** Eric White
**Client** I.L.S. Records

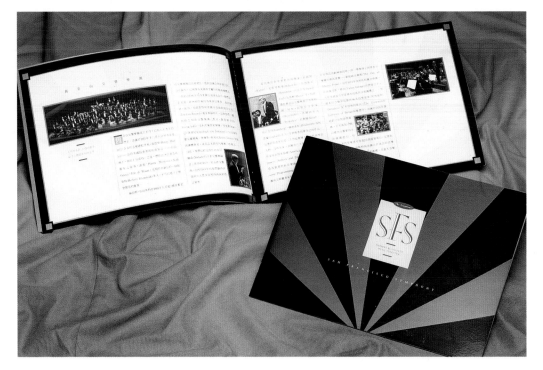

**Title**   San Francisco Symphony Identity
**Design Firm**   Leslie Chan Design Co. Ltd.
**Art Director**   Chan Wing Kei.Leslie
**Designer**   Chan Wing Kei.Leslie
**Client**   Amway Taiwan Limited

the Capitol Offense

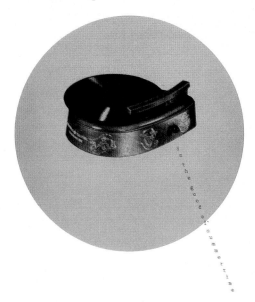

LOS ANGELES, CA

DOuble ScOOp SuMmer FuN

**Title**  The Capitol Offense Magazine Covers
**Design Firm**  Modern Dog
**Art Directors for Big Orange and Free**
  Jeff Fey, Michael Strassburger
**Art Directors for Trumpet Nose**
  Jeff Fey, Vittorio Costarella
**Art Directors for Double Scoop**
  Jeff Fey, Robynne Raye
**Designer for Big Orange and Free**
  Michael Strassburger
**Designer for Trumpet Nose**
  Vittorio Costarella
**Designer for Double Scoop**
  Robynne Raye
**Client**  Capitol Records

67

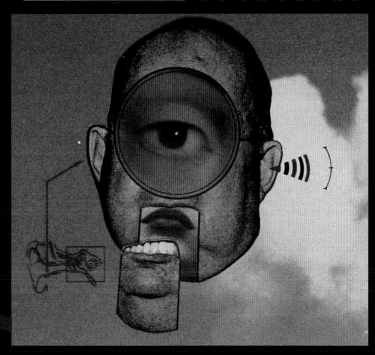

*absolutely*

*Left*
**Title**  Aural Fixations CD Packaging
**Design Firm**  PolyGram Records
**Art Directors**  Michael A. Klotz
**Designers**  Michael A. Klotz
**Client**  PolyGram Records

*Right*
**Title**  Sand Rubies/Goodbye CD Packaging
**Design Firm**  PolyGram Records
**Art Director**  Sheryl Lutz-Brown
**Designer**  Sheryl Lutz-Brown
**Client**  PolyGram Records

**Title** "Hitting the High Notes"
Poster and Invitation
**Design Firm** Sayles Graphic Design
**Art Director** John Sayles
**Designer** John Sayles
**Illustrator** John Sayles
**Client** Planned Parenthood

*absolutely*

**Title** Greta/Revolver CD Packaging
**Design Firm** PolyGram Records
**Art Director** Sheryl Lutz-Brown
**Designer** Sheryl Lutz-Brown
**Client** PolyGram Records

**Title**  Seattle Camerata Logo
**Design Firm**  Hornall Anderson Design Works
**Art Director**  Jack Anderson
**Designers**  Jack Anderson, David Bates
**Photographer**  Seattle Camerata
**Calligrapher**  Nancy Ogami
**Client**  Dali Records

**Title**  Kirk Alford/Piano Technician Logo
**Design Firm**  DogStar Design
**Art Director**  Rodney Davidson
**Designer**  Rodney Davidson
**Illustrator**  Rodney Davidson
**Client**  Kirk Alford

71

**Title**  Dewin Tibbs/Operatic Baritone Logo
**Design Firm**  DogStar Design
**Art Director**  Rodney Davidson
**Designer**  Rodney Davidson
**Illustrator**  Rodney Davidson
**Client**  Dewin Tibbs

*Top*

**Title**  Sneak Peeks Logo

**Design Firm**  Rebecca Sobaje Design

**Designer**  Rebecca Sobaje

**Client**  JMC Acquisitions, Inc.

*Bottom*

**Title**  Logo for K. Lee Scott, Composer/Conductor

**Design Firm**  DogStar Design

**Art Director**  Rodney Davidson

**Designer**  Rodney Davidson

**Illustrator**  Rodney Davidson

**Client**  K. Lee Scott

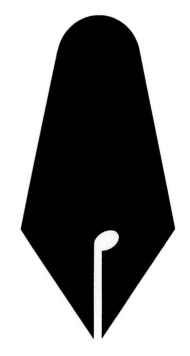

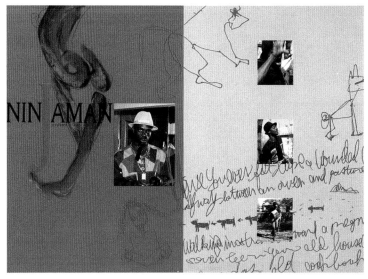

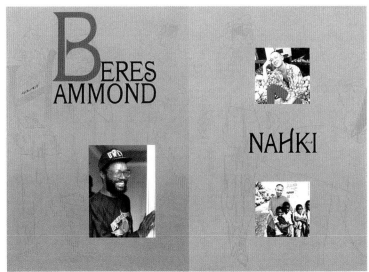

73

**Title** Reggae Japansplash Promotional Book
**Design Firm** Alfalfa Inc.
**Art Director** Takeo Aizawa
**Designer** Takeo Aizawa
**Illustrator** Shigeki Yamane
**Client** Tachyon Co., Ltd.

74

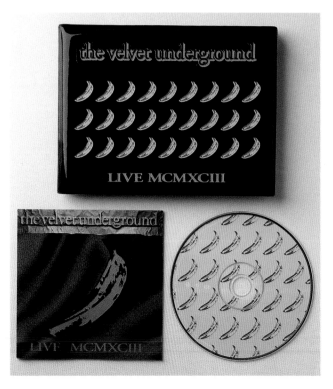

*absolutely*

*Top*

**Title** Live MCMXCII/The Velvet Underground –
Retail Poster and Limited Edition CD Packaging

**Design Firm** Just Design

**Art Directors** Sylvia Reed, Spencer Drate, Jeff Gold

**Designers** Sylvia Reed, Spencer Drate,
Jütka Salavetz, Dennis Ascienzo

**Photographer** Ted Chin

**Poster Production** Chloe Harrison, Andrea Delregno

**Client** Sire/Warner Bros.

*Bottom*

**Title** Warner Bros. 1993 Holiday Greeting Cookbook

**Design Firm** Modern Dog

**Art Director** Jeri Heiden

**Designers** Robynne Raye, Michael Strassburger

**Illustrator** Robynne Raye

**Client** Warner Bros. Records

*Left*
**Title** "Jazz Live at the Hyatt" Poster
**Design Firm** Sayles Graphic Design
**Art Director** John Sayles
**Designer** John Sayles
**Illustrator** John Sayles
**Client** Hyatt Newporter

75

*Right*
**Title** Wine & Food Showcase Poster
**Design Firm** Sayles Graphic Design
**Art Director** John Sayles
**Designer** John Sayles
**Client** Des Moines Metro Opera

76

*Left*

**Title** "Flaming Lips" Poster

**Design Firm** Modern Dog

**Art Director** Vittorio Costarella

**Designers** Vittorio Costarella

**Illustrator** Vittorio Costarella

**Client** Moe Cafe

*Right*

**Title** "Better Than Ezra" Poster

**Design Firm** Modern Dog

**Art Director** Vittorio Costarella

**Designer** Vittorio Costarella

**Illustrator** Vittorio Costarella

**Client** Moe Cafe

*absolutely*

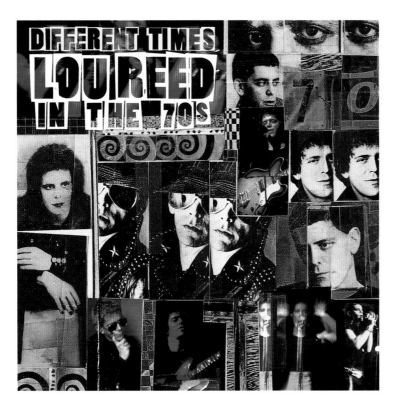

78

**Title**   Viva Italia!
**Design Firm**   Modern Dog
**Art Director**   Naomi Taubleb, RCA Records
**Designer**   Vittorio Costarella
**Illustrator**   Vittorio Costarella
**Client**   RCA Records

**Title**   Hello, My Name is...
CD Sampler for Music Convention
**Design Firm**   Modern Dog
**Art Director**   Jeri Heiden, A+M Records
**Designer**   Michael Strassburger
**Photoshop**   Michael Strassburger
**Client**   A+M Recoeds

# theat*RICAL*

## *absolutely*

**F**rom school plays performed in gymnasiums to vast productions with full orchestras and famous stars, live performances reach all types of audiences. All you need to create theater is a performer and a spectator—add music and you have dance; add illusion and you have magic; add marionettes and children and you have Saturday morning at a museum. The posters, logos, and promotions included here are some of the best work highlighting the performing arts.

81

**Title** "One Mo' Time" Poster
**Design Firm** Bartels & Company, Inc.
**Art Director** David Bartels
**Designer** David Bartels
**Illustrator** Gary Kelley
**Client** Monsanto Foundation

82

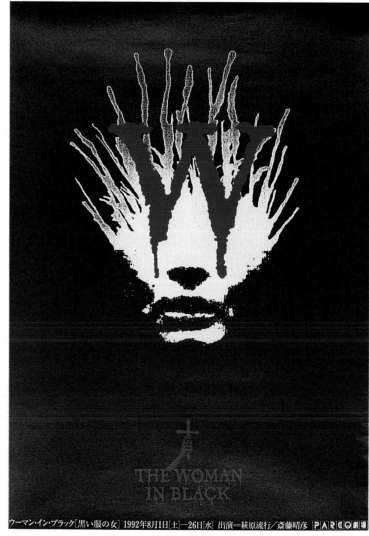

absolutely

**Title** The Woman in Black Poster Series
**Design Firm** Hiromura Design Office
**Art Director** Massaki Hiromura
**Designers** Massaki Hiromura,
 Nobuhiko Aizawa
**Client** Parco Co., Ltd.

ART LIBRARY

このセリフが、まるで天から降って来たかの様に私の頭に浮かび大いなる安らぎが私を包んだ。

私は、とり憑き離れない亡霊を断ち切る術は破り庭める事だと思いまして、そうだ。私も、破り庭めよう。あの話を語るのだ。私に書き記すのだ、あの忌まわしい眠りの生徒を払い、細大もらさず。私独自の幽霊の話を書くのだ。それでみんなも知り、私も永遠に破に済められ、語る事で記憶もよみがえる。最初の小麦着く事は終わらない、次は語ることだ。私は祈る、我々全てに、神の御加護があります様に。

暗転。俳優、誕生。

THE WOMAN
IN BLACK

ウーマン・イン・ブラック「黒い服の女」1992年8月1日[土]—26日[水] 出演—萩原流行／斎藤晴彦 PARCO劇場

84

*absolutely*

**Title**  Coppélia Program
**Design Firm**  Graphic Partners
**Art Director**  Ron Burnett
**Designer**  Andrea Welsh
**Illustrator**  Emma Parker
**Client**  The Scottish Ballet

85

**Title** Arlington's Arts al Fresco Logo Series
**Design Firm** Steven Morris Design
**Art Director** Steven M. Morris
**Designer** Steven M. Morris
**Client** Arlington County, Virginia Cultural
      Affairs Division

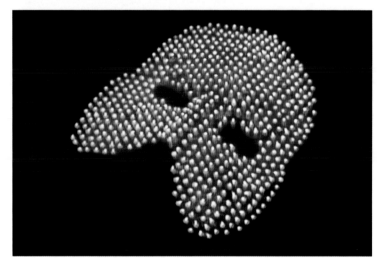

_absolutely_

**Title**  "Candles" Video for "Phantom"
**Design Firm**  Echo Advertising & Marketing Inc.
**Art Director**  Jerry Huckins
**Designer**  Jerry Huckins
**Copywriter for CD**  Rob Simpson
**Director**  Dan Izzard
**Client**  Live Entertainment Corporation

**Title**  Seasoned Performers Logo
**Design Firm**  DogStar Design
**Art Director**  Rodney Davidson
**Designer**  Rodney Davidson
**Illustrator**  Rodney Davidson
**Client**  Seasoned Performers

**Title**  Eugene Oniegan Logo
**Design Firm**  Sabin Design
**Art Director**  Kelly Davenport
**Designer**  Tracy Sabin
**Client**  San Diego Opera

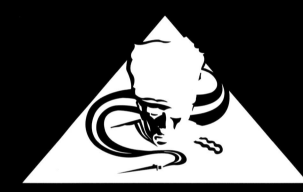

**Title**  Arts Alive Logo
**Design Firm**  Trudy Cole-Zielanski Design
**Art Director**  Trudy Cole-Zielanski
**Designer**  Trudy Cole-Zielanski
**Client**  Frostburg State University

88

**Title**  Wolf Trap Promotion
**Design Firm**  Supon Design Group, Inc.
**Art Directors**  Supon Phornirunlit,
　　　　　Andrew Dolan, Steven Morris
**Designer**  Steven Morris
**Client**  Wolf Trap Foundation for the
　　　　　Performing Arts

*Top*
**Title** "Giselle" Promotional Literature
**Design Firm** Graphic Partners
**Art Director** Ron Burnett
**Designer** Andrea Welsh
**Illustrator** S. Parker
**Client** The Scottish Ballet

89

*Bottom*
**Title** "Phantom" T-Shirt
**Design Firm** Gregory F. Scott
**Art Director** Gregory F. Scott
**Designer** Gregory F. Scott
**Client** Theater Under the Stars

*absolutely*

**Title** "Nutcracker" Campaign
**Design Firm** Richards & Swensen, Inc.
**Art Director** William Swensen
**Designer** William Swensen
**Client** Ballet West

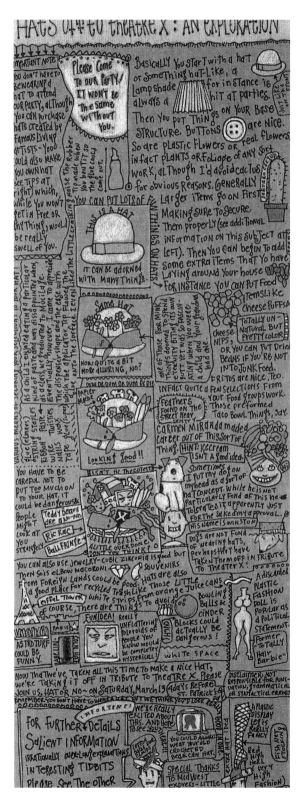

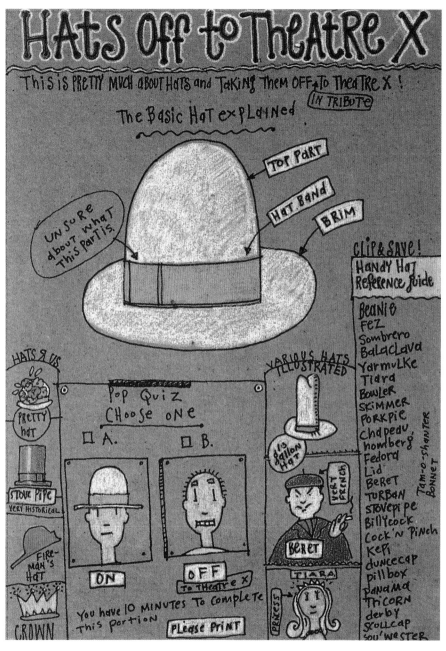

**Title**  Hats Off to Theatre X Poster
**Design Firm**  McDill Design
**Art Director**  Clayton Feller
**Designer**  Michael Dillon
**Copywriter**  Michael Dillon
**Client**  Theatre X

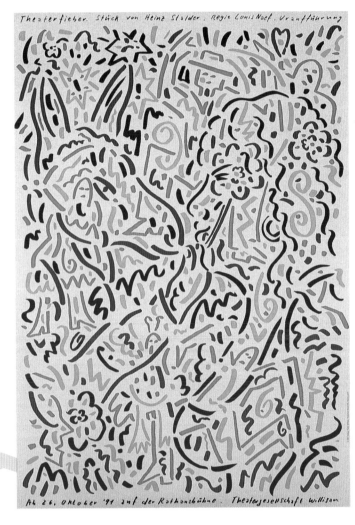

*absolutely*

*Left*

**Title**  Theaterfieber Poster

**Design Firm**  Niklaus Troxler

**Art Director**  Niklaus Troxler

**Designer**  Niklaus Troxler

**Client**  Kleintheater Luzern

*Right*

**Title**  Bil je skrjanec Poster

**Design Firm**  KROG

**Art Director**  Edi Berk

**Designer**  Edi Berk

**Client**  MGL (Town Theater of Ljubljana)

*Left*
**Title** "Love Letters" Poster
**Design Firm** Hiromura Design Office
**Art Director** Massaki Hiromura
**Designers** Massaki Hiromura,
Yoshiko Komatsubara
**Illustrator** Toshio Nomura
**Client** Parco Co., Ltd.

*Right*
**Title** Das Lachen Poster
**Design Firm** Niklaus Troxler
**Art Director** Niklaus Troxler
**Designer** Niklaus Troxler
**Client** Mad Theater, Bern

93

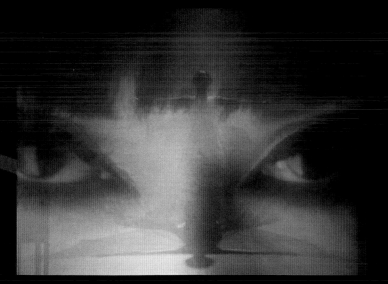

**Title** "Kiss of the Spider Woman" Video

**Design Firm** Echo Advertising & Marketing Inc.

**Art Director** Jerry Huckins

**Designer** Jerry Huckins

**Copywriter for CD** Rob Simpson

**Director** Vincent Paterson

**Client** Live Entertainment Corporation

1993 THE
BOLSHOI
BALLET
SCHOOL

*Top*

**Title**   Bolshoi Ballet School Brochure
**Design Firm**   Hiromura Design Office
**Art Director**   Massaki Hiromura
**Designers**   Massaki Hiromura,
            Takafumi Kusagaya
**Client**   The Seiyu, Ltd.

95

*Bottom*

**Title**   25 Jahre Kleintheater Luzern Poster
**Design Firm**   Niklaus Troxler
**Art Director**   Niklaus Troxler
**Designer**   Niklaus Troxler
**Client**   Theatergesellschaft Willisau

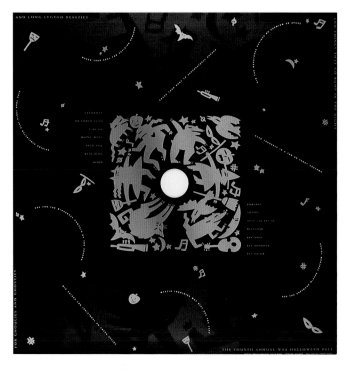

*absolutely*

*Left*

**Title**  Washington Software Association
Halloween Ball Poster

**Design Firm**  Hornall Anderson Design Works

**Art Director**  Jack Anderson

**Designers**  Jack Anderson,
Julie Tanagi-Lock, Lian Ng

**Client**  Washington Software Association

*Right*

**Title**  "Kaj je Resnica" Poster

**Design Firm**  KROG

**Art Director**  Edi Berk

**Designer**  Edi Berk

**Client**  MGL (Town Theater of Ljubljana)

absolutely

*Left*

**Title**  All in the Timing Poster

**Design Firm**  Modern Dog

**Art Director**  Robynne Raye

**Designer**  Robynne Raye

**Illustrator**  Robynne Raye

**Client**  Seattle Repertory Theatre

*Right*

**Title**  Foetus Poster

**Design Firm**  Modern Dog

**Art Director**  Michael Strassburger

**Designer**  Michael Strassburger

**Illustrator**  Michael Strassburger

**Client**  Tasty Shows

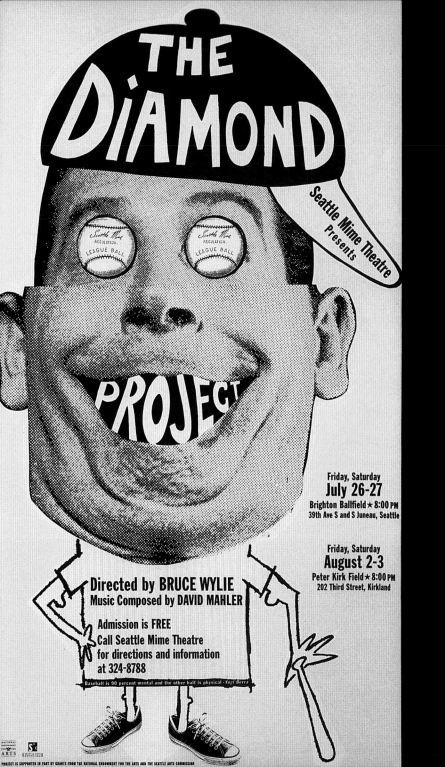

**Title** The Diamond Project
**Design Firm** Modern Dog
**Art Director** Robynne Raye
**Designer** Robynne Raye
**Illustrator** Robynne Raye
**Client** Seattle Mime Theatre

# miscelLANEOUS

## absolutely

**A**nything that brings people together with the intention of amusing them, but doesn't fit into our previous four categories, is included here. Art festivals, craft fairs, carnival celebrations—even the occasional bird-calling contest—all fall under our general entertainment umbrella, along with pumpkin-hurling contests and hayrides. In most cases, the only thing these graphics have in common is that they are as entertaining as the events they promote or support.

**Title**  29th Bird-Calling Contest Poster
**Design Firm**  Bartels & Company, Inc.
**Art Director**  David Bartels
**Designer**  Brian Barclay
**Photographer**  Tom Ryan
**Client**  Piedmont High School

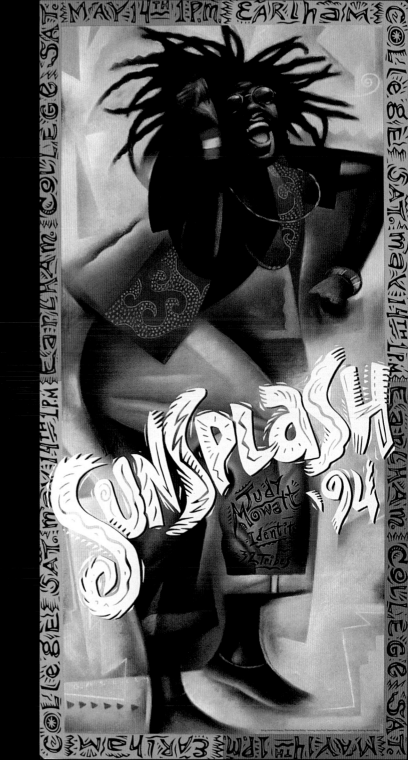

102

osolutely

**Title** Sunsplash '94 Poster
**Design Firm** Bartels & Company, Inc.
**Art Director** David Bartels
**Designer** Aaron Segall
**Illustrator** Gary Kelley

**Title** Full-Color Flyer
**Design Firm** Adriana Cortazzo
**Art Director** Adriana Cortazzo
**Designer** Adriana Cortazzo
**Client** Mister Good Bar

104

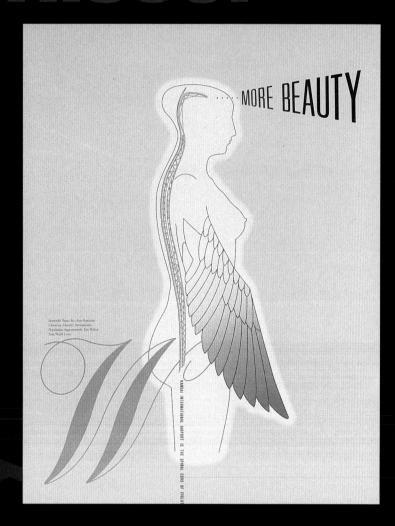

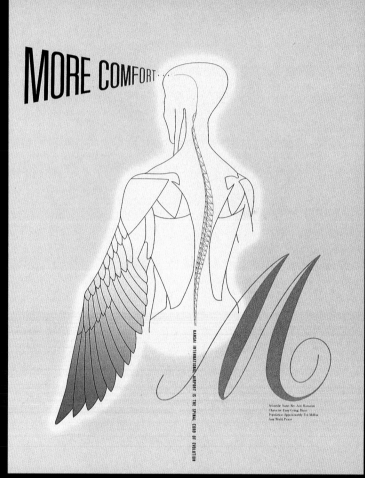

**Title**   More Comfort and More Beauty Posters
**Design Firm**   Tad Co., Ltd.
**Art Director**   Takashi Matsuura
**Designer**   Takashi Matsuura
**Client**   Osaka Design Center

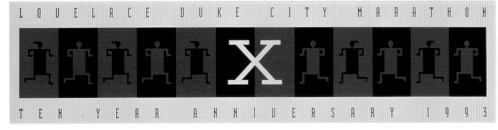

*Top*

**Title**  Rail Fair Poster
**Design Firm**  The Dunlavey Studio, Inc.
**Art Director**  Michael Dunlavey
**Designer**  Lindy Dunlavey
**Client**  California State Railroad Museum

*Bottom*

**Title**  Duke City Marathon Poster
**Design Firm**  Vaughn Wedeen Creative
**Art Director**  Rick Vaughn
**Designer**  Rick Vaughn
**Computer Production**  Chip Wyly
**Client**  Duke City Marathon

106

*Left*
**Title**  World Cup Pocket Guide
**Design Firm**  Supon Design Group, Inc.
**Art Directors**  Supon Phornirunlit,
            Andrew Dolan
**Designer**  Steven Morris
**Client**  ISM (Soccer) Inc.

*Right*
**Title**  Fremont Fair Poster
**Design Firm**  Modern Dog
**Art Directors**  Vittorio Costarella, Al Parisi
**Designer**  Vittorio Costarella
**Client**  Fremont Public Association

Us convidem a la inauguració
del nostre bar Cue* Sant Cugat,
el dijous 30 de setembre de 1993,
a partir de les 20 h.
Us hi esperem!

Carrer St. Martí 12. (a 50m. C.A.P.-Creu Roja)
Sant Cugat del Vallès. Tel. 589 47 90

107

**Title** Cue Sant Cugat Invitation
**Design Firm** Sonsoles Llorens
**Art Director** Sonsoles Llorens
**Designer** Sonsoles Llorens
**Client** Cue Sant Cugat

*absolutely*

*Left*

**Title**  Artstorm Poster
**Design Firm**  Hornall Anderson Design Works
**Art Director**  Jack Anderson
**Designers**  Jack Anderson, David Bates
**Client**  Downtown Seattle Association

*Right*

**Title**  Shiki Soku Ze Ku Poster
**Design Firm**  Tad Co., Ltd.
**Art Director**  Nobuyo Kataoka
**Designer**  Nobuko Kataoka
**Copywriter**  Kisoji Otori
**Photographer**  Hideo Aomatsu
**Client**  Osaka Design Center

Dig fun in the sun?
SandJam's the one!
Build a castle and play
you're king for a day!

Just DIG IT

SAT AUG 6TH

SAND JAM '94
SAT, AUG 6TH
BIG CREEK
STATE PARK

BUILDING 11 Dr 53 FT
28 AUG '94 481 YARDS 5 INC

110

**Title**  IBM's Olympic Sponsorship Identity
**Design Firm**  Supon Design Group, Inc.
**Creative Director**  Lee Green
**Art Directors**  Supon Phornirunlit,
          Andrew Dolan
**Designers**  Andrew Dolan, Andrew Berman
**Illustrator**  Andrew Dolan
**Client**  IBM

*absolutely*

36 USC 380

IBM®

*Worldwide Information
Technology Sponsor*

36 USC 380

IBM®

*Worldwide Information
Technology Sponsor*

© 1995 IBM Corp.

© 1995 IBM Corp.

112

*absolutely*

**Title**   Expand Your Horizon
**Design Firm**   Sayles Graphic Design
**Art Director**   John Sayles
**Designers**   John Sayles
**Illustrator**   John Sayles
**Client**   Fort Dearborn

113

**Title**  Iowa Department of Tourism Logos
**Design Firm**  Sayles Graphic Design
**Art Director**  John Sayles
**Designers**  John Sayles
**Illustrator**  John Sayles
**Client**  Iowa Department of Tourism

114

*absolutely*

**Title**   The Hit Parade and Ballyhoo,
        The Sweet Cuisine of Broadway
        Promotions
**Design Firm**   John Brady Design Consultants
**Art Director**   Mona McDonald
**Designers**   Rick Madison, Mark Murphy
**Illustrator**   David Bowers
**Client**   March of Dimes, Pittsburgh Chapter

**Title** Toga Party Invitation
**Design Firm** CarverLetcherMiller
**Art Directors** Tom Carver,
William Letcher, Bill Miller
**Designer** William Letcher
**Client** Caesars Palace

# inDEX

### ART LIBRARY

116

design FIRM